Donald Ayres' EXMOOR

DONALD AYRES

HALSGROVE

First published in 2001 by Halsgrove
© 2001 Donald Ayres

ISBN 1 84114 123 2

British Library Cataloguing-in-Publication-Data
A CIP data record for this book is available from the British Library

HALSGROVE
Halsgrove House
Lower Moor Way
Tiverton EX16 6SS
T: 01884 243242
F: 01884 243325
www.halsgrove.com

Printed and bound in Italy
by Centro Grafico Ambrosiano

Contents

My thanks to Andrew and Tina Stockman of the Strand Gallery,
Brixham, for all their help and encouragement.

This book is dedicated to Tony Crook of the Barle Gallery, Dulverton. His faith in my work over many years and his assistance in the final preparations have made it possible.

Donald Ayres

The sun glinted on the Bristol Channel and the gentle curve of Porlock Bay swept round to Bossington Head. I sat in a sea of heather, sketchbook in hand, almost too entranced to do anything. The fields along the shoreline were a patchwork of warm greens and gold and the air hummed with insects. A huntsman with half a dozen hounds galloped across my line of vision. It was 1977 and my love affair with Exmoor began.

A long series of events had led to this moment. I entered the world on 28 September, 1936, in a small south-coast town called Bexhill-on-Sea, the first baby to be born in the newly opened hospital.

I was an only child and lived with my mother and grandmother. My first memories are of my grandmother's house in Highfield Gardens, Sidley. It was one of half a dozen along a small unsurfaced lane backing on to Sidley railway station which was little more than a halt on the branch line linking Bexhill with the London to Hastings main line at Crowhurst. Many a happy hour was spent watching the steam trains pass by the end of the garden. The railway bridge led to a footpath that crossed some fields, through a farmyard complete with duckpond and ducks to the open countryside beyond. This was the countryside that nurtured my love of distant, open landscape, of muddy tracks, five-bar gates, trees and hedgerows. Even at the age of three I loved it so much my mother used to call it my farm.

There were no other children nearby so I had no friends and was essentially a lonely child. Drawing my own stories kept me occupied and probably set me on the path to being an artist. Some genetic talent must have been there as my mother was of artisan stock. She was a dressmaker, her father a basket-maker and music and artistic talents were scattered amongst various aunts, uncles and cousins.

My father came from and worked in the East End of London so I hardly ever saw him. When the war began he went into the fire-service there. As a result it was a complete stranger who appeared, when I was nine years old, to butt in between my mother and me. We never got on together for the rest of his life. I suppose that, in modern phraseology, we never bonded.

Most of my early memories are, of course, to do with the war. I was just three when it began. I remember the hit-and-run raids of the German planes that appeared without warning to bomb and strafe. Bexhill was where the German invasion was expected. The pathetic strings of barbed wire on the beach and widely spaced gun emplacements I doubt would have stopped a single armed tank. At night the bombers flying overhead to go and blitz London kept me awake. It is a sound that still sends shudders through me when I hear recordings of it.

The South Downs, 1940. A painting based on childhood memories.

Soon after I started school my mother and I moved to a council house. It was only half a mile away from my grandmother and Number Three of twelve semi-detached buildings in a small cul-de-sac surrounding a tiny green which, although it was round, was called the Square. On one side was a single, old-fashioned lamp-post. In the front garden of the house was a filled-in bomb crater and there were bullet holes up the wall. Almost every other house contained children, most within a year or two, of my own age evenly split between boys and girls. The sensitive, artistic, five-year-old loner had to change quickly or be bullied mercilessly. I opted to become one of the gang.

My mother was not a sociable person. She kept to herself and had no real friends other than my aunts and uncles. There was very little parental supervision for either me or my friends so, out of school, we ran wild. The biggest danger came from the skies and there was little any parent could do about that. The best hope of survival was to recognise the sound of friend from foe and be ready to dive for cover. What our parents could not have realised was what we got up to; playing in

bombed-out buildings, collecting live rounds of ammunition and hiding in hollowed out haystacks to smoke cigarettes we had scrounged from the Canadian soldiers billeted on families round and about.

Later on came the doodlebugs, heading for London but often falling short and nearby. For one summer I was taken away from it all to stay with relations of my father in Dumfries in Scotland where my cousins

Sussex coastline, 1940

looked upon me with envy because they had never seen a German plane. To this day I can draw a Spitfire pretty much from memory.

The war ended when I was nine. My father came home. Everything changed. I was all that he did not want in a son and nothing for which he had hoped. I realise now that with his background, having an artistic son meant only one thing – probably his worst nightmare. He tried to make me take up boxing and was always on about making a man out of me and sending me into the army as soon as I was old enough. He did, however, take us away from the council estate and bought his own house at a time when it was rare for one of his background. Eventually he got involved in his own life and responsibilities and, apart from the occasional outburst, left me alone.

School was nothing special. I shone at art, loved history, swimming and gymnastics and didn't give a damn about anything else.

I had always wanted, when I left school, to be an artist but it was pounded into me that nobody made a living as an artist and you had to get a 'proper' job. Despite this I managed to get myself accepted by Hastings Art School but just at the point where I was about to start I had another row with my father and he refused to sign the papers unless I did what he wanted. I was a minor, supposedly at his whim, but I was in no mood for supplication. With my artistic talents I had been offered a job as an apprentice diamond setter by a man who, before the war, had been a top jeweller in Hatton Garden and had helped to reset the Imperial Crown for the 1936 Coronation. I told my father to shove his authoritarianism and took the job. It was a misjudgement. I was an outdoor person and though I may have spent the long winter evenings drawing and painting, in the summer any spare moment was spent in the sea or exploring the countryside either on foot or bicycle. Being shut in a workshop for long hours as a lowly apprentice was boring beyond belief.

After one year I had had enough. I was in no mood to come to terms with my father so to my mother's distress I left home and joined the Royal Navy. This was a move I did not regret. By the time I was seventeen I had travelled half the world and seen the last gasps of the British Raj. I had taken part in the last great Spithead Review for the 1953 Coronation where ships of the Royal Navy covered the sea to the horizon. I had been on the fringes of the Malayan Campaign for which I received a medal although my part in this brave encounter was putting up the fairy lights over the ship in readiness for the Queen's birthday celebrations!

On the cruiser *Newfoundland* I encountered George Deakins who will be well remembered on Exmoor for his years in his gallery in Dunster. In those days he was a gunnery officer and having his first exhibition in Singapore. I did a fair amount of art-work in my Navy days but not what I wish now I had done. I experienced the end of an era but at that time it seemed eternal and in no need of record. Instead, I drew naked women for the crew!

For two years I was shore-based at Portland in Dorset. There I met my future wife, Ann, a student at Weymouth Teacher Training College. Our courting was done in Radipole Park and freezing on Weymouth Pier despite which the relationship survived and we were married in 1958.

After two years at the Portland Anti Submarine Establishment, H.M.S. *Osprey*, it was decided by the Navy, in its wisdom, that I should 'volunteer' to become a submariner and I was sent to H.M.S. *Dolphin*, the submarine training school. I finished my training, got married and for two years barely saw my wife at all. In September 1960 I bought myself out and faced the nasty shock of being a civilian in the hostile world of London.

In those days Social Security was not an option. You got a job or were a social pariah. My wife's parents with whom we then had to live were very aware of their, and by association our, respectability. I was not qualified for anything. I spent six months selling encyclopaedias door-to-door and living with her parents on my wife's income as a teacher.

Luckily, a series of flukes led to my getting a job with an advertising firm and we were able to rent a decent flat in Beaconsfield, Buckinghamshire, where things began to look up. In 1962 our first child, Michael, was born and I bought our first house, in Sittingbourne, Kent.

During our four years in Sittingbourne I began drawing and painting again. Felt pens were the new thing. Ann bought me one and I made a lot of sketches of the old barges and creeks of the Thames Estuary at Faversham, Sheppey and along the north Kent Coast.

Early felt pen drawing, Kent

Broadstairs was another favourite place. But one day I ate a crab sandwich that made me seriously ill for several weeks and unable to work. Sickness benefit was £4 per week, our expenses were £30. In an attempt to make ends meet Ann took some of my sketches to a local shop one Thursday morning and persuaded the owner to put them in their window. On Friday evening she passed the shop and they were nowhere to be seen. She came home very upset but before she could leave on Saturday morning to sort things out a letter arrived which read, 'I saw your pictures in the shop on Thursday but when I went back on Friday they had all gone. I would like you to do one especially for me.'

Another three people knocked on the door the same day with similar requests. It was the start of my career as a 'real' artist.

I began getting commissions to draw and paint people's houses and sometimes their boats. Kent was richly endowed with timber-framed cottages and old manor houses. One time I was paid in apples by a local farmer. Galleries all around Kent began to take an interest. I was doing less and less work for the firm and more and more for myself. With the consent of my wife I turned to painting full time.

At this point I decided that it was time to get some serious training and went, for a while, to both Canterbury and Maidstone art schools. Unfortunately I got nowhere. There was nobody to teach me the skills and techniques that I wanted to learn. The phrase at the time was 'Action Painting' and its main proponent was known for laying a large board on to the floor of his studio, throwing down buckets of paint and riding over it on his bicycle. A wise man who had been through the system told me to forget the art schools.

'If you go down that path it will destroy your natural talent.'

I took his advice and spent many hours in London galleries studying the Old Masters and making copious notes on their techniques. My favourites were the Victorian and Albert Museum and the Wallace Collection. I was especially influenced by the landscapes of the Dutch Schools and the English Victorians.

It was 1965. A conflict arose in me. There we were living the lifestyle of 'young executives' – another phrase of the time – on an estate of social climbers, trying desperately to be the 'respectable' people desired of us by our parents. I was an artist. We had been to Paris, to Montmartre, we had tasted a little of the bohemian lifestyle. We were not really respectable. Again, with my wife's consent, (bless her) we decided to abandon the rat race. We sold our house and with Ann now pregnant with our second child moved to Cornwall.

For me, the main attraction was, 'Cornwall – The Artist's Colony'. We rented a tiny little flat in an idyllic position. It was a two-and-a-half-room residence over the ships chandlers shop by the river at Fowey. There was no kitchen, just a galley in the corner of a small living room; a bedroom barely big enough to take a double bed; a box room that was filled with Michael's cot, and a bath that was only big enough to sit in. But the window of the living room filled the entire wall and overhung the river. The first impression was of green water lapping beneath and wooded banks on the far side. Directly opposite was the ferry slip at Bodinnick

with the Du Mauriers' house by its side and the narrow village street and picturesque cottages disappearing up the hill. Looking up the river from the window we could see the jetties of the china clay port and every so often the bulk of a tramp steamer would fill the window as it glided past. Once, one got into difficulties and had to be turned by tugs. Its bow came so close it blotted out the daylight. I loved it.

It was May 1966. There was nowhere to park the car so I got rid of it and bought a small boat. How times have changed. I went to the Harbour Master to ask where I could moor my boat. He pointed to a position just 100 yards from our flat.

'Anywhere around there,' he said. 'You wait until the tide is right out.

You bury a cast-iron railway sleeper, (that you can get from the abandoned railway line) in the mud, attach a chain, line and buoy and that's all there is to it.'

It did not cost a penny! A second-hand, five-horse-power seagull motor took us noisily on exploration trips up wooded creeks to hidden villages and to picnics at little coves only accessible by boat. The summer drifted by like a dream. The place was filled with artists and writers with whom I made friends. We talked, drank and partied, sat in the sun, swam in the sea, sailed, danced the Floral Dance, sat amongst the fireworks as they drifted down the river at the climax of the regatta and, oh yes, very occasionally painted a picture.

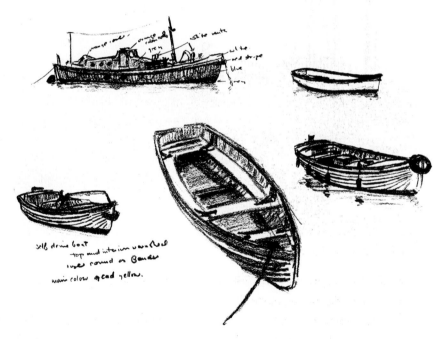

In October our second son Kim was born in the tiny bedroom of the flat which now seemed very small indeed. I managed a few paintings during the winter but out-of-season Cornwall was not interested. I had expected to continue doing house and boat portraits but nobody wanted them. Things looked tricky. Trading some pictures for the hire of a car saved our bacon by enabling me to visit galleries in Bath and the Cotswolds. Unfortunately it was not enough and our money had all gone. Then to our surprise Ann became pregnant again. Not to worry. Summer came round again. Between changing our boat for a larger sailing one, swimming and generally enjoying ourselves, I earned a very modest living selling sketches and watercolours of Fowey, Polperro and Mevagissey. We lived on mackerel which was very easy to catch and the local shopkeepers were very helpful. The bank manager was not. He came to the door and demanded my cheque book back.

Another incident occurred which could so easily have been the end of me. I had a very good friend called Peter who worked part-time for the local boatyard and lived on his boat on the river. It was a lovely old gaff-rigged fishing boat called *Morgan-le-Fey*. He had rescued it from a mud flat and restored it himself. He had helped me with the repairs of my own boat and often came to us for meals. One day when he was with us a knock came at the door. The message was that a man in the pub on the quay had a crewing job for Peter. Having nothing better to do I went with him. It was an ex-naval man and there was an immediate rapport between us. He took us out to his boat moored off Polruan, a large Scottish MFV equipped for salvage work. He was going on a treasure hunt. He knew of a secret wreck and although he hinted at all sorts of things it was very hush-hush. The salvage laws in those days were that once you were outside the 12-mile limit you were beyond the law. If the big boys caught a whiff, anything could happen – even murder. So I didn't know what or where it was.

'Come with us,' he said to me.

I had felt the movement of the boat under me the moment I stepped aboard and the memories of my life at sea came rushing back. I wanted to go. I really wanted to go. We went over to Polruan for tea with his wife and afterwards I went home, full of enthusiasm, to tell Ann. For once, she said no. She was heavily pregnant, unwell and she wanted me there. I stayed at home.

'Look after my boat,' said Peter and off he went.

Some months went by. We heard nothing but made weekly trips to *Morgan-le-Fey*. One night in the autumn there was an horrendous south-easterly gale which blew straight into the harbour. Everybody in Fowey was down at the water, watching. The next morning Peter's boat was cast up on the beach, totally wrecked. A few weeks later the Harbour Master told me that the salvagers had been caught by that big storm near the Channel Islands and all had been drowned.

During that summer of 1967 I made the lengthy trip by bus and train across Cornwall to Newquay. I took three or four oil paintings under my arm and went round the galleries. The Newquay Gallery, run by a Mr Robertson, was the largest and situated over the baker's shop. He bought my pictures but I looked at the hundreds of others thinking that mine would be lost amongst them. To help with the finances Ann took a job as an usherette at the local cinema but eventually had to stop when the ice-cream tray was resting too heavily on the baby's head! The summer drew to a close, the next baby was due and the flat was desperately cramped. We needed to move but I was already a couple of months behind with the rent and could not afford to buy paints. There was no work. Another knock at the door. Mr Robertson from Newquay was standing there wanting some pictures. I didn't have any.

'Paint some.'
'I have no money.'
'How much do you need?'

He pulled out what I remember as a huge wad of notes. He paid the rent. He paid for the move. He paid for some paints and canvasses. I shall always remember him with affection for that act of faith.

We moved to an old farmhouse on the edge of town called Lawhyre Farm. It is now holiday cottages but then it was a working farm with one half of the house converted for holiday lets. We took it for the winter.

Lawhyre Farm

My daughter, Coralie, was born in November. This time, because of feared complications, Ann had to go into hospital in Plymouth. Coralie was fine but Ann was there for three weeks and very poorly for several weeks afterwards. I had to look after her, take and collect Michael from school, cope with one-year-old Kim and care for a newly-born baby. It did not leave much time for painting. I appealed to the Social Services for help.

'Get a job.'

You could not register as unemployed when you were self-employed. I could not take a job even if offered one or what would have happened to Ann and the children? Eventually they relented and awarded us a home-help twice a week for whom we had to pay. Mr Robertson came over weekly to collect the paintings. I bought an ex- butcher's bicycle with the huge basket on the front. I was now mobile but it was like peddling a tank. We survived another winter – just. With the approaching spring we had to move. Nowhere was available. Summer visitors would be taking all available lets. Once more, a knock upon the door. Another saviour. The solicitor who had dealt with the sale of our house in Sittingbourne and whose portrait I had painted had come to see how

I was getting on. He happened to have a bungalow, which he rarely used, in the village of Chilsworthy near Gunnislake on the Devon, Cornwall border. We could have it for as long as we liked. I swapped my boat for a clapped out old Morris Minor that just got us to Chilsworthy before it gave up the ghost entirely.

Chilsworthy was an intimate little village on a hill overlooking the Tamar Valley. The distance was dominated by the western tors of Dartmoor. It could all be seen from the window of the bungalow. We soon got to know everyone in the village. Michael went to school in Gunnislake. I used to ride him to the top of the hill in the basket of my bike so that he could catch the bus. During this period I continued to sell my pictures to Newquay. I made some contacts in Plymouth and painted the portrait of the Mayor of Lostwithiel. I also loved exploring the valley beneath us. The river Tamar wound through it and hidden in the woods were dozens of old mine shafts and overgrown, ruined engine houses from the tin mines. We stayed there for about six months. Time for change came when my mother died suddenly from a heart attack. I decided to make an attempt at reconciliation with my father.

I spent a month painting local pictures and then held an exhibition in the bungalow for the villagers. Everybody came and bought something. I made £400 – quite a lot for those days. It paid for us to move to Bexhill-on-Sea. On a quick trip there I had found us a large maisonette to rent over the top of Dorothy Perkins in Devonshire Road in the centre of the town. Ann took the babies and went on the train. The removal firm we had booked to come down from Kent broke down and never arrived. I had to find a local firm who would come at the last minute. I travelled to Bexhill with five-year-old Michael in the front seat of the removal van. It seemed to take forever. We arrived at one in the morning and then had to unload it all. That is one move that I will not forget. I did not exactly forge a good relationship with my father. He thought I was a wastrel. But at least I felt he could get to know his grandchildren. Because we lived in the town centre we were a convenient resting place for all our friends and had many visitors. My father came often.

Painting-wise it was a disaster. Our first months in Bexhill were probably the worst. The kind of pictures I had painted in Cornwall were totally unsuitable for the South East. To help with the finances Ann took a job washing up at a local private school. Her money paid the rent and fed the children. We ate the leftovers from the school. We opened up the fireplace and every day Ann took the pushchair to the beach to collect driftwood for us to burn – we could not afford coal. But with the spring came a new optimism. Instead of painting quick, slick sketches I took a month out to paint one picture. When it was finished I took it to the best gallery that I could find, Stacy Marks in Eastbourne. He bought it and wanted more. My career had taken a new turn. I returned to my original premise and made frequent trips to the National Gallery, the Tate, the V. & A. and Greenwich where I studied the Old Masters in depth. That first summer in Bexhill was glorious. The sun came out at the beginning of June and stayed out until the end of September. I worked from eight in the evening until four in the morning and slept all day on the beach. Other galleries began to take an interest in my new work including some in London. It was 1968, the height of the swinging sixties and the air was full of optimism.

The next change came when by chance I met a Dutchman with the unlikely name of Fred Van Dyke. He was an art dealer and had recently opened a gallery in Eastbourne.

'Work for me in the gallery,' he said, 'and paint pictures of the South Downs. I will pay you £30 per week.'

I had a job! The national average wage at the time was £20 per week so I was not doing too badly and it was regular.

Then my father became ill and died unexpectedly. He left his house to the woman who had moved in as his housekeeper after my mother had died. My mother had always said that if she died first I would get nothing which turned out to be the case. I did get a couple of hundred pounds, on the proviso from the solicitor that it would only be forth-coming if I did not contest. At the time that amount paid the legal fees which with my new job enabled me to get a mortgage on a modest house. So I took the money and did not contest the will. It has rankled me ever since.

The house I bought had potential. I borrowed £1000 from the bank and did it up. Now I was a house-owner and respectable again. I even had a cheque book again. I was friendly with a local estate agent and with his guidance sold the house within six months at double the price. I was confident. I had learned my trade. I could sell my paintings anywhere. It was 1972. I could live wherever I liked. House prices were shooting up. I decided to keep going west until I got ahead of the boom and then buy. And that is how I came to Wales.

After a series of chance events we bought a house in the village of St. Clears on the Carmarthenshire, Pembrokeshire border in west Wales. For £5000 we had five bedrooms, three large reception rooms and an enormous attic room with gigantic oak beams that I turned into my studio. The locals thought we had paid through the nose; it had been on the market for four years and we could have got it for half the price. But we lived in that house for nine years, longer than anywhere else before. Coralie began her schooling in Wales and was soon talking happily in Welsh The local headmaster was a keen amateur artist and became a good friend. The River Taf ran through the centre of St Clears dividing the village into upper and lower. It was further divided by church and chapel, still further by Welsh-speaking and non-Welsh speaking, Conservative and Liberal and yet again by locals and incomers. It is surprising that anybody spoke to anybody else but somehow it all seemed to work. Laugharne, where Dylan Thomas lived and died and wrote Under Milk Wood was just 5 miles away. I think that says it all. I like to feel that we were accepted. We joined in village life and participated in local events.

For the first few years in Wales life went by pleasantly and smoothly. My income increased and came steadily from galleries in London,

Birmingham, Stratford-upon-Avon and the Cotswolds. I had my first ever oneman exhibition at the Queensway Gallery in Birmingham. We had an acre of garden, separate from the house but down by the river, and Pendine Sands, just nine miles away, was a favourite place for a quick trip to the seaside. We often went for long walks with the children along the Pembrokeshire Coastal Path and over the hills. Eventually Michael went to school at Llandovery College so we spent a lot of time at the Brecon Beacons and deep in the Welsh countryside.

I had, from time to time, painted a few hunting scenes. They were done principally because the red coats and hounds made a colourful contrast to the predominantly green landscape. They were not of any hunts in particular but two were published as prints, one by a company that soon went bankrupt and the other by a major art publishing house. I was not paid for either and it was my first encounter, although unfortunately not my last, with the sharks of the art world.

Fate then threw up one of those events that seem to happen to me. At the back of our house was a small dirt lane and a couple of whitewashed stone cottages, one of which was bought by a couple called Steve and Mary. Steve was the whipper-in for the Carmarthen Hunt and before long was taking me to the meets and explaining the finer points. As a result, my hunting pictures became more authentic and popular, leading to a chance meeting in Bristol with Keith Gardener of the art publishers and dealers, Michael Stewart Fine Art who commissioned me to paint six pictures which he sold immediately. He then offered me a contract – they would buy everything that I painted.

About a year earlier we had taken the children for a holiday to Butlins at Pwhelli. It was fun for the children and for the first time in years Ann and I could have time alone together. We explored Snowdonia and had a wonderful time. We decided to repeat the experience the following year and went to Butlins at Minehead. The rest, as they say, is history.

The scene mentioned at the beginning with Dennis and the tufters led to a series of Exmoor-based hunting pictures. *Across The Moor* impressed Keith and his partner Paul Cooper so much that they decided to publish it as a Limited Edition Print. It became the most popular and lucrative print that I ever did but they sold the original painting to Keetches Gallery in Exeter who put it in their window and sold it the same day. It has not been seen since.

There was something about Exmoor that entranced me. The heather moorland, the wooded coombes, the rocky streams, the panoramic vistas, the presence of the sea never far away, cast a spell on me. I loved it all from the start. I have been told that Exmoor is notoriously difficult to either paint or photograph but to me it has never been a problem. The only comment I can make is that I understand the shape of the land. It goes back to the farm of my childhood, to the many cycling and painting trips across the South Downs. It was the land of the Doones with their secret places that captured my child's imagination so strongly. My very first trip across Exmoor was on a coach from Weymouth when Ann and I were courting. On our way to Lynton and Lynmouth the coach driver pointed out Doone Valley and Oare church, 'where the bullet hole is still visible in the wall'.

So in 1977 when we took the children to Butlins at Minehead one of the first things we did was to drive to Malmsmead and walk up Badgworthy Water to Hoccombe and back round to Lank Combe. It was magic – a Doone behind every tree. To this day it remains one of my favourite parts of the moor and I have painted it many times.

One of the problems with modern, everyday life is that the car makes us lose our sense of scale and perspective in the landscape. Twenty miles is a distance you cross in half an hour, not a day's hard trudging. It is easily forgotten that almost within my lifetime Porlock and Countisbury hills were unmade roads because they were too steep for steamrollers. My father-in-law used to tell us of illegal hill trials there on his motorbike when he was young man in the twenties. So when I walk along Badgworthy I see it as it should be, as it was, an out of the way path on the edge of a wilderness. When I was a child and my friends and I used to explore the woods and the marshes of East Sussex, we would pretend and partly believe that we were the first people ever to set foot on this remote spot. It evoked a sense of wonder. That sense of wonder remains to this day on Exmoor. When I returned to Sussex a few years ago and found that 'my farm' was now an endless stretch of housing estates bisected with a bypass, it distressed me beyond measure. That sense of oneness with the land is something I recapture when I walk the combes of Exmoor or sit on the riverbank with my paints. It is so precious. Recently an artist friend of mine, Terry Burke, and I were discussing the proposal by commercial interests of knocking down some old parts of Brixham.

He said, 'These people don't seem to realise that you can't buy antiquity.'

I would say the same of the moor. You can't buy wilderness either.

I am not a hunting, shooting or fishing man. Without the traditional country sports the landscape would change. There would be no cover kept for pheasants, no copses to nurture foxes and as they are such destructive beasts, no deer on Exmoor. Country sports made the English landscape. They also are, largely, the keepers of it.

In 1976 I was offered a job teaching at Carmarthen Art College twice a week. Three years earlier they had begun a wildlife illustration course, the only one of its kind in the country and the brainchild of Julian Brown, a senior lecturer there. They had full-time lecturers to teach graphics and design and visiting experts on wildlife. My function was to teach painting techniques – one day with the third-years and one day with the fourth-years. At the beginning I found the students were frustrated and rebellious. They were nearly all experts themselves on wildlife and did not want to bother with graphics and design – they wanted to paint wildlife. It took a while to win them over. I did it eventually, I think because I stood before them with an easel in front of me and said, 'This is how you do it,' and then took them through the painting

stroke by stroke – an unheard of act. It became very rewarding when at the fourth-year Diploma Exhibition Melissa, who had produced an excellent picture, was photographed for the newspaper and said when I congratulated her, 'I had a very good teacher'.

Because of my own frustrations with art school I could understand where they were coming from.

We went camping and youth-hostelling together and in the summer I took them to several idyllic locations along the Towy Valley where we would paint and sometimes swim. I was surprised to see from my diary at the time how many of them would come to my house when they felt like it for help and advice. The most talented were also the most rebellious and were not liked at all by most of the staff but Mrs Hancock who was head at the time backed me in preventing several of them from being expelled.

In 1977, Michael Stewart Fine Art published my Exmoor painting, *Across the Moor* with another called *Gone to Ground*, along with a couple by another artist. This was a time when the country was coming apart at the seams with numerous strikes. The prints were due for release in late summer but Paul Cooper who was organising the publication met frustration after frustration. There were several delays on mine due mainly, according to the printers, to power cuts. They were eventually promised for October, then November and finally December. The proofs were okayed and delivery was promised for 22 December. Paul invited me to his home to sign them but when I arrived, still no prints.

'This afternoon definitely!' said the printers.

Paul took me to his local for lunch and a couple of pints after which I did not really care. Half of the prints arrived late in the afternoon and somehow I managed to sign 250 of them. Then Paul and his wife took me for more drinks and on to an Italian restaurant. I stayed with them for the night but the next morning there were still no more prints. The printers

River Tawy Donald Ayres '73.
For Ann.

were on strike over a dispute about their Christmas bonus and would not guillotine the last batch. Paul, ever the sharp one, went straight to the printers and paid the man on the guillotine his Christmas bonus himself and we had the rest of the prints by lunchtime. Paul is a generous host and I signed them in an alcoholic haze having to be reminded of my name on a few occasions. *Across the Moor* was almost an instant sell-out with most of them selling through the Barle Gallery at Dulverton.

This led to a demand for original paintings of Exmoor and in the summer of 1978 I took my caravan and stayed at a very pretty campsite at

Bridgetown. It was in a wooded valley with the River Exe on one side and an old mill and mill stream on the other. Mr and Mrs Sherring ran the site. They had one of the prints of *Across the Moor* and made us very welcome. I had my first meeting with Tony and Joan Crook of the Barle Gallery who were keen to have my originals of Exmoor and Tony arranged for me to meet Norah Harding who was a Joint Master of the Devon and Somerset Staghounds. She showed me over the kennels, introduced me to Dennis Boyles the huntsman and arranged for me to follow the hunt in her Land Rover. I had several trips out with the Devon and Somersets in this fashion. In between meets with sketchbook in hand I travelled as much of the moor as I could. It was an exciting time. I remember that nearly everyone to whom I was introduced said, 'Oh yes, I have a print of *Across the Moor.*'

Throughout the winter I found that I could put to good use all that I had learned during the summer and half of the pictures I painted were of Exmoor. Another print was discussed and there was talk of an exhibition at Dulverton. Michael Stewart Fine Art wanted to do two more prints of mine and I was taken to meet Colonel Berkeley of the Berkeley Hunt. I had days out with them and trips with the Clifton Beagles of which Keith Gardener was the Master. Tony Crook arranged for a cottage to be let to me and my family at Dulverton during the Easter holidays. For two weeks I was out on the moor painting, sketching and going out with the hunts. Captain Ronnie Wallace invited us to his house. He was Master of the Exmoor Foxhounds and Chairman of the Association of Masters of Foxhounds, internationally renowned as the modern-day 'Field Marshall of foxhunting' and much in demand throughout the world as a judge of hounds.

A brief extract from my diary at the time:

'*Mrs Harding fixed up for me to go in the Landrover with Frank Holloway. The weather was near perfect. The sun was shining and at last it felt like spring. There were hundreds of people at the meet both on horses and in cars. I did some sketching, took some photographs and went to find Mr Holloway. Whilst I was looking someone gave a speech about the Labour party's manifesto to ban hunting and urged everyone to write to their MP. Frank and his Landrover were parked out on the fringes of the crowd. When the field moved off we were near to the front and followed along the top of Molland Common to the point where the hunt proper began. As usual everything was watched from distant high points through field glasses. Four stags were sighted, one was singled out and the chase began in earnest. We went in pursuit. We charged along muddy tracks and over bogs at what seemed like 60 miles an hour. It was so fast the Land Rover didn't have time to sink...*'

I made several more trips in the backs of Land Rovers for both staghounds and foxhounds. With the foxhounds I travelled with Lawrence, the terrier man. I saw many parts of the moor this way that I would otherwise have missed. In August of that year the exhibition was held at the Barle Gallery that further cemented my relationship with Exmoor. Over the following couple of years I made frequent visits. During the school holidays I stayed in the caravan at the Sherrings campsite and at odd times in between, when Keith wanted me to do something in particular, I would drive to his home near Bristol and the following day we would go to either Exmoor or the Quantocks to follow the hunts. More limited edition prints followed, including the *Devon and Somersets at Hawkcombe Head, The Dulverton Country* and one of Captain Wallace with the Exmoor Foxhounds.

Away from Exmoor Chay Blythe commissioned me to paint his favourite hunt – the East Cornwall. I also painted the Berkeley and another of Keith's own hunt, the Clifton Beagles. I had a one-man exhibition at Harrods in London and my paintings appeared in and on the covers of *Field, Country Life, Shooting Times* and *Hounds* magazines.

My connection with the art college led to an interesting aside. I went to Scotland to an estate near Dornock to paint a Grouse Hawking party. Only one painting came out of it but it was an interesting view of a more unusual country sport.

As the new decade got underway I began to get the urge for pastures new. I had lived in St Clears for longer than anywhere else since I had left home. The art school moved to a bigger building in the grounds of Trinity College and was calling itself, rather grandly, the Dyfed College of Art. The group of students I had seen through almost their entire course had left and my enthusiasm began to wane. Also I began to feel less at home in Wales as it became more nationalistic. Although we personally never felt any unpleasantness, it was a time when second homes belonging to the English were being burned down and everywhere were constant reminders that the English were not welcome. Even signs in both languages with Welsh at the top had the English parts painted over. The final straw came when I applied for outline planning permission to build a new house on my land by the river and was refused for a trivial reason. Someone offered to buy my house and I agreed. We moved to Devon in September 1981.

I was torn then, and still am, between the desire to live on Exmoor and what I fear would happen if I did. I have lived in many places in my life and I know from experience that no matter how wonderful one feels about a place to begin with, sooner or later one begins to take it for granted and then stops seeing. One of the joys for me is that each time I return to Exmoor I see it with fresh eyes. I am sure that it shows in my work.

The sea is also very important to me so we moved to Brixham. I love the character of Brixham and as there were now six of us, Ann, myself and three teenage children, plus Michael's girlfriend from Wales, we found a five-bedroom house with an extra room for a studio at the top of the hill, midway between Brixham and Kingswear, with views across the whole of Torbay in one direction and out across the Channel in another. Kim and Coralie continued their schooling in Dartmouth. Within a few months we realised our mistake. Parking in Brixham is almost impossible. To enjoy the town you have to be within easy walk of the harbour. We found that we never went there. We did our shopping in Paignton which at that time I did not even like although I have

changed my mind since. We put our house on the market in 1982 just as the recession of that time began and the housing market died. So, almost, did the picture market. Added to that hunting was becoming very politically incorrect and galleries stopped exhibiting hunting scenes for fear of upsetting their clients. I continued to visit and paint Exmoor on a regular basis but for my livelihood I had to look elsewhere. I was saved in this case by another art dealer by the name of Mike Chafen. He was one of the great characters of the art world at the time and it would take a book in itself to tell of him. He was busy making connections in Germany. The Germans were the rich men of Europe. My relationship with Mike led to several shows in Frankfurt and painting trips through the Black Forest, Bavaria (a wonderful place) along the Romantic Strasse, down the Rhine and through many medieval towns.

It was now the mid-eighties and suddenly the economy took off like a liberated horse, taking me and everyone else along with it. The children began to leave home. We sold the house and bought a fisherman's cottage in Brixham with wonderful views across the harbour. With the motorway I could get to Exmoor in less than one and a half hours. I had the best of all worlds. But as often happens, the gods love to kick the ladder from under me when I am doing well (although they tend to put it back when things get dire). I became involved with two art dealers (who shall remain nameless) who promised me the earth but practically destroyed me. One was a charmer who I found later was a con-man. I have since met several people who lost all their savings to him. I discussed his offers with Alwyn Crawshaw who said that it all sounded too good to be true so probably was! How right he was but at the time I found that what was on offer was too hard to resist. Unbeknown to me I had provided paintings that gave him the authenticity to be an art dealer. I was lucky in that he paid me well for everything I produced but the promises he made and the failure to deliver wound me up to such an extent that I began to have health problems which still pursue me today. At the same time Ann's father died. Her mother needed to be looked after and our house in Brixham was totally unsuitable so once again it was time to move.

View from my Studio in Brixham (1987)   Oil   20 x 24in

I wanted to get as far away from everything as possible so in May 1988 we moved to Scotland, to Dumfries and Galloway where I opened my own gallery at the stately home of Drumlanrig Castle. It was a fortunate move as in the next recession during the nineties nearly every art dealer I know went to the wall. Because for the first time in my life I was selling my work directly to the public I survived. My years in Scotland are another story. I continued to visit and paint Exmoor but not as often as I would have liked. In the spring of 2000 it became time to put Scotland behind me and return to Devon.

My relationship with Exmoor has now renewed itself with vigour.

Eilean Donan Castle, Scotland Oil 20 x 30in

Painting Techniques

These are just a few hints, tips and advice with a brief description of how two of the paintings in this book were done. If what I describe is a little oversimplified it is because to go through the process in detail would require a book to itself. I hope therefore that any aspiring artists will be able to understand at least some of what I have to say.

When I say that the first stage is to pick a subject, this is not as obvious as it sounds. In general the subject finds me. I spend a lot of my time travelling and **looking**. Over the years I have learned to recognise what in my opinion would make a good painting. I know of more subjects than I could possibly paint. I say this because the response of many leisure painters is to rush out and get a postcard or a book of photographs and think, 'That is a lovely subject. I'll paint that.'

Believe me, when they do that it shows. There is nothing wrong with using photographs but they must be your own photographs that you took yourself. I cannot emphasise enough the importance of having been there, to have breathed the air and felt the atmosphere, of knowing what is to the left, to the right, behind the photograph. The confidence imparted by this gives the painting authenticity. Better yet is not just to photograph but to sit back and sketch as well. Even a small, simple sketch will implant something of what you feel about the scene into your brain that nothing else can because during the act of sketching you have to really look at the subject.

Moleschamlee

Look at the sketches of Turner. Of his many hundreds most are simple in the extreme but they enabled him to produce great art. Even better is to do a small painting. I most often use watercolour for this. If you must use photographs remember that this is the scene at only a fraction of a second. Remember also the old saying, 'It is not what you've got that matters – it is what you do with it.'

The second stage is to get the composition right. For simplicity's sake I recommend the simple S shape. The basic contours follow the S shape and lead the eye through the picture.

SIMPLE S SHAPE COMPOSITION.

Most of the paintings in this book are done in either oil or acrylics. For many years, like many others, I had dismissed acrylics out of hand as somehow not quite real art, not cricket. Recently I have begun to change my mind because I have found that I can do with acrylics techniques that I was never able to achieve in oils and certainly not in a reasonable time scale. The Old Masters used to have assistants to do all the mundane jobs and worked on an entirely different time scale from the one we would use today. I can do in acrylics, in a few days, a painting which, if I had done in oils to a comparable level, would have taken me months. I delight also in being able to work on one painting from its beginning to conclusion without having to wait days, if not weeks, for each stage to dry. Therefore the following demonstrations are done in acrylics.

Fancy boxes of paint and equipment are not going to turn you into a good artist. Invest your money in a handful of best quality brushes and no more than a dozen artist quality paints. Best quality synthetic brush-

es are ideal for acrylics. I use about ten different brushes at any one time. I recommend three or four watercolour type brushes: a rigger, a size 0 or 1 for fine lines, a size 5 or 6 and a large flat varnishing type brush. The latter becomes even more useful when slightly worn. The rest should be a mixture of hard, flat brushes in sizes 1, 3, 5 and possibly 12.

For colour it is best to think in terms of the colour wheel.

Cold Yellow – Cadmium Yellow pale (or lemon)
Warm Yellow – Cadmium Yellow medium (or deep)
Cool Red – Cadmium Red deep
Warm Red – Cadmium Red medium
Cold Blue – Ceroleum (or Monestrial Blue with great care)
Warm Blue – Ultramarine
As much Titanium White as you can afford to buy

These are all you need to create a masterpiece but some earth colours are useful if you want to be more versatile:

Naples Yellow
Yellow Ochre
An earth red (Red Oxide, Venetian Red)
Burnt Sienna
Burnt Umber

I have done some of my best work using only the following three colours and white:

Yellow Ochre
Cadmium Red deep
Ultramarine

If you must have green use the muted Green Oxide of Chromium. Having any more colours will make painting more difficult, not easier.

For a palette, a simple sheet of white paper is all that is necessary. For your medium – a jam jar of clean water.

TIP: *buy an empty plant spray bottle, fill it with water and periodically give your paints on the palette a quick spray. This will prevent the acrylics from drying too quickly.*

I paint on MDF board primed with Acrylic Gesso Primer. It will outlast any canvas and for me it is the ideal painting surface.

TIP: *Get your local hardware store to cut you two-dozen 8 x 10in pieces and prime them all in one session.*

ADVICE THAT YOU PROBABLY WON'T TAKE:

With ten of your prepared boards beside you, your subject to the front and a generous amount of paint at your side, jump straight in and paint with as much confidence and abandon as you can muster. Don't worry about the details just block in the shape and basic contours. Allow yourself five minutes then set the board aside and repeat the process with the next board. Look at your subject through screwed-up eyes to block out the details. Do not take it seriously – it is meant to be fun! When all the boards are dry pack them up and take them home. A week later get them out and look at them. Choose the best one and begin adding any details that you think are necessary. You may be surprised at the result.

1

Demonstration 1

1) On a primed 16 x 12in MDF board I drew, with a pencil, the few lines that position the basic shapes of the picture. I filled in the simple areas with mid-tone colours. It is best not to be too precise or careful at this stage. I added plenty of white and sky blue to the colours as I moved into the distance with more texture in the foreground. The mid tones are the block of colours you see when you squint through half closed eyes to block out the details.

2) Now I started to add some simple shape to the forms by loosely brushing some slightly deeper mid tones for the shadows and slightly lighter mid tones for the areas facing towards the light. For the shadows I use cooler colours, adding Blue mixed with Burnt Umber. For the lighter areas I used warmer tones of Cadmium Yellow.

2

3) I have added more detail still following the principles outlined above. The beauty of using acrylics is that at this stage you can change shapes and recede tones and details. When I paint I feel my way along bit by bit. I do not work to any set pattern or formula. I work until it looks right but I do this stage by stage so that the painting comes together as a whole and not piece-by-piece.

4) Again, more of the same. More detail. Some darker darks and lighter lights. A hint of heather, stones on the path and contours on the hills.

People say to me, 'How do you know when it is done?'

My response is that knowing when it is done is the most difficult part of painting a picture. I often work in the company of several other artists. We have all been painting professionally for at least thirty years. All of us still, on occasion, go too far and refer to it as 'over-cooking' the picture. But if you recognise that you have gone too far you can always back track and paint out unnecessary detail. Ultimately, the artist is the only one who can decide at which point he is going to stop. You may have noticed that I have refrained from using the word, 'satisfied'. No artist worth his salt is ever satisfied. That is what drives him on to paint a better picture the next time. That is how he progresses. Any artist that I have met who thinks he is a great artist is precisely the opposite.

Demonstration 2

1) As before I drew in just the basic shapes in pencil. The beauty of pencil is that it can be erased. If you draw it in with a brush in acrylics you can't (unless you are very quick) because the unwanted lines can show through the paint. The mid tones of the sky, hills, trees etc. are all blocked in. When I begin a painting I have in my mind an image of how I want it to finally appear. The rest of the process is the struggle to get down on to the canvas or board the image I saw in my mind.

2) Shadows begin to appear and outlines of distant trees and hedgerows. In Britain, every distant view is seen through a mist. Sometimes it may be a very thin haze but no matter how clear the atmosphere, it is always there to a greater or lesser degree. When painting a landscape creating that effect is fundamental to its success. When painting, think 'fog'. As it recedes the colours are paler and bluer. Cool colours recede and warm colours come closer.

3) This is a close up detail showing how the cottage and field patterns are progressing but not yet finished.

4) Another detail. When applying the paint in the blocking stage I put the pigment on thickly and worked it over with a big, softish brush to give texture. When I put on the next layer of lighter colour the texture helps the surface to be more interesting.

5) We are back to knowing when the painting is finished. For me it is when it looks something like the image I had in my head. It is never as good. Occasionally it gets close. On those occasions I allow myself a little satisfaction.

All great works of art contain certain ingredients in common: good composition, the best possible balance of light and darks and a great combination of warm against cold colours. In the hands of the master chef the subject matter is immaterial. Abstract art developed from this premise. Its aim was to produce great works with all the ingredients in place but the subject matter abstracted and simplified almost out of existence. Some stunning results were created and as an artistic experiment it opened new doors to the artistic imaginations of artists around the world. Unfortunately, two things happened. Those elite beings who are richer, smarter and more fashionable than the rest of us were quick to grasp the possibilities of an art form that was not easily understood. Quick to join them were the many wannabe artists who found the disciplines of traditional artistic skills too demanding. Encouraged by the elitists they used their superior numbers to take over the art schools and art establishments and systematically destroyed centuries of skills and technical knowledge. Painting as an art form is now considered a relic of the past and the traditional, professional artist has become an endangered species.

Young people who would have had the talent to extend the boundaries of traditional art find themselves frustrated and now turn to other disciplines where genuine creativity is highly prized. I am thinking particularly of the burgeoning world of computer graphics, of films and games. It seems that is where most of the talent has gone.

We are left in the art world of today with the idea that a work of art is not valid unless it is backed by a theory; where the idea is more important than the work itself and where the fashion is for the emperor's latest outfit. I would like to paraphrase the famous American writer Tom Wolfe: a picture is worth a thousand words but if a thousand words are needed to describe a picture then it has surely failed.

The Paintings

Near Pool Bridge in Wilmersham Wood
Acrylic 16 x 12in

Across the Slopes at Dunkery
Acrylic   16 x 12in

❖

In 1966, I nearly took a cottage at Worthy, just a few hundred yards up the Toll Road. I often wonder how different things might have been had I moved to Exmoor then instead of ending up in Cornwall. I remember the words, 'Full Repairing Lease' as being the deciding factor in the choice. Over ten years passed before I rediscovered Exmoor.

❖

Porlock Weir
Acrylic   16 x 12in

View from Bossington Hill with Luccombe Church and Dunkery Beacon
Acrylic 16 x 12in

The Danesbrook
Acrylic 16 x 12in

The Danesbrook
Acrylic 16 x 12in

❖

*A beautiful spring morning. We had stayed the night before at the Fo'c's'le
Inn on the beach at Combe Martin. Yellow gorse blossom was everywhere.
This particular view is from near Martinhoe looking down on Woody Bay.
The Valley of the Rocks is in the far distance.*

❖

Exmoor Coast
Acrylic 16 x 12in

Bossington
Watercolour 6 x 4in

Study for a painting of the River Barle near Landacre
Oil 5 x 7in

Study for a painting of Winsford Common
Oil 5 x 7in

Study for a painting of Porlock Bay from across Horner
Oil 5 x 7in

Study of West Anstey Common
Oil 5 x 7in

Study of a scene near Cussacombe Gate
Oil 4 x 5in

Dennis Boyles Blowing to Hounds
Oil 28 x 36in

Porlock Bay
Oil 16 x 20in

Gundogs
Oil 16 x 20in

East Water Valley
Acrylic 16 x 12in

High Exmoor Vista near Brendon Two Gates
Acrylic 16 x 12in

Robbers Bridge
Acrylic 16 x 12in

❖

This to me is the heart of Exmoor. To get to this particular spot you follow the footpath up from Lorna Doone Farm at Malmsmead to the bottom of Hoccombe combe. To an imaginative person there is a Doone behind almost every tree. It is one of my favourite places.

❖

Badgworthy Water
Acrylic 16 x 12in

River Barle near Withypool
Acrylic 16 x 12in

Tarr Steps
Acrylic 16 x 12in

Pool Bridge
Acrylic 16 x 12in

Exmoor Glade
watercolour 6 x 4in

Study for a painting of Winsford Common
Oil 5 x 7in

❖

It was a gorgeous spring day. The air was clear and the whole panorama visible to the horizon of the distant Chains. Gorse was in bloom everywhere. Hidden in the wooded combes below is the famous Hunter's Inn.

❖

View from near Trentishoe
Acrylic 16 x 12in

Study for a painting of Dunkery Beacon
Acrylic 5 x 7in

Dunkery Beacon
Oil 8 x 10in

Study of a view from Ley Hill
Oil 8 x 10in

Study of moor near Cussacombe Gate
Oil 5 x 7in

❖

*Set against the panorama of this Exmoor combe that leads the eye across Porlock
Vale, the Somerset and Welsh coasts to Steep Holm in the Bristol Channel.
It was painted as a formal portrait of the Devon and Somerset Staghounds
and shows many of the main members of the time including the Joint Masters,
Norah Harding and Michael Robinson with huntsman Dennis Boyles.*

❖

Hawkcombe Head
Oil 24 x 48in

Badgworthy Water
Oil 16 x 20in

Bluebell Wood
Oil 16 x 22in

Valley of the Rocks
Acrylic 16 x 12in

Badgworthy Water
Acrylic 16 x 12in

Badgworthy Water
Acrylic 16 x 12in

River Exe near Exebridge
Acrylic 16 x 12in

Doone Valley and Malmsmead from County Gate
Acrylic 16 x 12in

View from Dunkery looking across Horner to Porlock Common
Acrylic 16 x 12in

❖

Its claim to fame, of course, is where Lorna Doone was shot at her wedding. Where, a coach driver once told me, 'You can still see the bullet hole in the wall!' Also of interest to me was that after painting the picture I found an old photograph that I had taken whilst on that self-same coach trip in 1957 and it is amazing to see how much of the moorland has since been put to the plough.

❖

Oare Church
Acrylic 16 x 12in

Lee Bay
Watercolour 6 x 4in

Study of the Barle near Withypool
Oil 5 x 7in

Study of Anstey Common
Oil 5 x 7in

Study for a painting of Dunkery from Cloutsham
Acrylic 5 x 7in

Study of Dunkery Beacon
Acrylic 5 x 7in

❖

For me this view is the epitome of Exmoor. The Weir Water draws the eye up the valley to the high moor. At every turn in the path you long to see what is around the next corner. It almost sucks you into it.

❖

Weir Water
Oil 20 x 40in

Study for a painting of Dunkery
Acrylic 5 x 7in

Stag in Badgworthy Water
Oil 36 x 24in

Porlock Common seen from Ley Hill
Acrylic 16 x 12in

Dunkery seen from Ley Hill
Acrylic 16 x 12in

Dunkery from near Cloutsham
Acrylic 16 x 12in

In Porlock Vale
Acrylic 16 x 12in

❖

I went to Lynmouth to paint Watersmeet. Unfortunately it was at the height of
the foot and mouth epidemic and the whole area was closed off. Although it was
against 'my religion' I paid to go up the Lyn Gorge instead. We had to wade
through disinfectant to get there but it made my journey worthwhile.

❖

The Waterfall in the Lyn Gorge
Acrylic 16 x 12in

Dunkery Beacon
Acrylic 16 x 12in

Looking towards Minehead and the Coast from Dunkery
Acrylic 16 x 12in

Fallen Tree, Horner
Watercolour 6 x 4in

Study of Winsford Common
Oil 5 x 7in

Study for a painting of the Danesbrook
Acrylic 5 x 7in

Study of a scene near Stoke Pero
Acrylic 5 x 7in

Pony study
Acrylic 5 x 7in

Study for a painting of Farley Water
Acrylic 5 x 7in

❖

The Joint Master of the Exmoor Foxhounds admonishes an errant hound.
The background is of the combes of Horner Wood and the distant high moor.
To me it is another of those combinations of events and places that
are the essence of Exmoor.

❖

Jack Hosegood
Oil 20 x 40in

Dulverton Country
Oil 20 x 30in

Staghounds in Badgworthy
Oil 20 x 30in

View from Ley Hill
Acrylic 16 x 12in

Porlock Vale
Acrylic 16 x 12in

Oare Water
Acrylic   16 x 12in

Hawkcombe Head
Acrylic 16 x 12in

View from Wilmersham Common (pair)
Acrylics Both 16 x 12in

❖

I consider this one of my major works. It depicts Captain Ronnie Wallace one of the most famous hunters of our time and Master of Exmoor Foxhounds. Also in the painting are the joint Master Jack Hosegood and huntsman Anthony Adams. Behind them lies the Deer Park and Badgworthy Water, the area immortalised by R.D. Blackmore as Doone country.

❖

Exmoor Hunt
Oil 24 x 36in

Tarr Steps
Oil 16 x 12in

Old Houseboat, Porlock Weir
Watercolour 6 x 4in

Study of a scene beneath Dunkery
Acrylic 5 x 7in

Study of Winsford Common
Oil 5 x 7in

Study of Dunkery Beacon
Acrylic 5 x 7in

Study of Winsford Common
Oil 5 x 7in

Study for a painting of Badgworthy Water
Oil 5 x 7in

The Slopes of Dunkery
Oil 24 x 18in

Across Horner to Dunkery
Watercolour 6 x 4in

Study of Winsford Common
Oil 5 x 7in

❖

Dennis Boyles and the Tufters of the Devon and Somerset Staghounds gallop across Porlock Common. It was my first limited edition print and put my work before a much wider public across Exmoor and beyond. Not surprisingly this particular painting holds a special place in my heart.

❖

Across the Moor
Oil 20 x 40in

Study of Knighton Combe
Oil 4 x 5in

Study of the River Barle
Acrylic 5 x 7in

Study of Badgworthy Water
Acrylic 5 x 7in

Study of Winsford Common
Acrylic 5 x 7in

Wilmersham Common
Acrylic 7 x 5in

Oareford
Watercolour 6 x 4in

Exmoor Farm
Oil 16 x 12in

Landacre Bridge
Oil 16 x 12in

Badgworthy Water
Oil 16 x 12in

Devon and Somerset Staghounds
Oil 16 x 12in

Devon and Somerset Staghounds
Oil 16 x 12in

Devon and Somerset Staghounds at Hawkcombe Head
Oil   16 x 12in

Devon and Somersets on Porlock Common
Oil 16 x 12in

Porlock Weir
Acrylic 16 x 12in

Exmoor Stream
Acrylic 16 x 12in

Subscribers

Mr B. Abbotts, Birmingham
Kathy Adkins, Harlow, Essex
Jenny and John Allaway, Minehead, Somerset
Joan E. Allen, Tonbridge
C. W. and P. J. Allen, Cirencester
Noel Allen, M.B.E., Minehead
Dr James Appleyard
J. H. Arnold, Milverton
Marjorie G. Ayres, Bampton
Kathleen Ayres, Bampton
Anthony Ayres, Winchester
A. W. J. Baker, ex Winsford, Somerset
Mrs Jennie Bale, Ilfracombe
Jean and John Ball, Whitstable, Kent
Carole L. Ball, Maundown, Wiveliscombe,
    Somerset
P. J. Barber, Bristol
Esther Barefoot, Pilton
Joyce A. Barker, Somerby
Ethel Barnard, Dulverton, Somerset
Naamah J. Barnes, Blue Anchor
Lynda E. Barrett, Swansea
Paul J. Barrett, Stoneleigh, Coventry/Exford,
    Somerset
Richard Barron, Middle Burrow, Timberscombe
Keith Batchelor, Blandford
Mrs Patricia C. Bawden, Withypool, Somerset
Irene Bell, Brixham, Devon
Ian Martin Bell, Gloucester
George F. Bethel, California
Artie and Angie Biles, Foxearth, Loxbeare,
    Tiverton, Devon
Chris Binnie, Brockwell, Wootton Courtney
Malcolm and Annette Bond, Steeple Ashton,
    Wiltshire
David Bonney and Victoria Herriott, Exford
Hope L. Bourne, Withypool
Michael W. Bray, South Molton
Rebekah V. E. Brinkley, Triscombe Farm,
    Wheddon Cross
Madeleine L. E. Brinkley, Triscombe Farm,
    Wheddon Cross

Sarah A. Broom, Milverton
Raymond J. Brown, Cottles Farm, Woodbury,
    Devon
Mercia and Jim Brown, Saffron Walden
Ian and Pat Buick, Minehead
Joan Bunyan, Chapel Cleeve
Joan Burnell, Minehead
K. J. Burrow, Bucks Cross
Annabel M. Campbell, Sampford Brett
Fred Carter, South Molton, Devon
Jennifer and Leonard Chamberlain, Beer, Devon
Wendy A. Charman, Surrey
Sally Chilcott, Westbury, Wilts.
Dan and Glen Clark, St Audries
Sheila A. Clark, Potterspury
Sid Clench, formerly of The Coffee House
Mrs J. E. Clennel-White, Brimfield Common
Adrian Cockcroft, San Jose, California
Nick and Margo Cockcroft, Weymouth, Dorset
Mr Edward Colquhoun, South Molton, Devon
Graham W. J. Cook, Great Sampford
Mrs A. C. Cook and Mrs M. Nicholls, North
    Devon
Mrs M. Coveney, Welford-on-Avon, Warwickshire
Rosemary Cox, Willett House
Mr and Mrs Richard Crabb, Exford, Somerset
Steve Creech, Allerford, 2001
David Crudge, Burgess Hill
Peter J. Cunningham, Hertfordshire
Mrs Janet Curtis-Hook, Minehead
Gill and Philip Darlow, Reading
G. David, Bathpool
Aubrey and Joan Davies, Dulverton
Barbara P. Davis, Woodcombe
Thomas E. Day, Great Torrington, Devon
Mr and Mrs M. Deakin,
Jane and Karen Dennis-Smither, Simonsbath
John S. Dewell, Blue Anchor
Marjorie Dixon, Ennerleigh
Andrew Dixon, Bishops Lydeard
Brian J. Duke, Simonsbath
Ralph N. Eales, Ashill

Cyril J. Easton, Washford
Neville Eckley, Holcombe Rogus
Tony Elbourn, (for his parents)
Tina Fagan, Tolland
Lady Farrington
David J. Fennell, Barnstaple
A. M. (Nita) Ferrar, Cottingham, East Yorkshire
Jean B. Ford, Alcombe
Eileen Forrest, North Molton
Joan Foster, Pirbright, Surrey
Robin Foster-Brown, Dulverton
Gillian Fox-Spencer, Five Bells, Watchet, Somerset
Mr and Mrs N. J. Frape, Kuwait
Mr Paul S. Gammin, Paignton
Muriel Gapp, Torquay, Devon
Caroline J. Giddens, Minehead
Mike and Josie Goldsmith, Checkendon
Alyson Govier, Brompton Ralph
Arthur J. Greedy, Wiveliscombe
Geoffrey and Diana Green, York
Roger Gregory, South Molton
Nigel Grinstead, Pitsford Hill
Andrew W. Guscott, Okehampton, Devon
Patricia Hadland, Barrington, Somerset
Maggie Hamlin, Minehead
Kay Patricia Hammond, Broadstairs, Kent
Jonathan M. Hawes, Enfield
Michael Lynton Haycraft, Swinderby, Lincoln
Michael Heard, Tiverton
Mrs Shirley Hibberd, Ilfracombe
Penny Hogg, Exford
Keith and Pat Hole, Brompton Ralph
Peter Hollands, Malvern Wells, Worcestershire
Rosemary Hufton, Reigate
Mr and Mrs P. Hull, Dulverton
Peter Hulm, Singapore
Christopher P. Humphries, Launceston, Cornwall
Major D. Ide-Smith
Reginald W. Jaggers, Braunton
David G. Jemmison, North Molton
Scarlett Jukes, Cothelstone
Sally N. Kemp, Brompton Regis

Mrs Janet Kift, Lee, Devon
Dorothy M. King, Old Hunstanton
Martin and Judy Kingdon, South Molton
Mrs J. Kinton, Bournville
Mrs S. A. Knifton, Bexhill-on-Sea
Margaret J. Knight, Landkey
Mr Martyn R. Knight, Taunton, Somerset
J. H. Lambert, Wheddon Cross
David and Jackie Latham, Porlock, Somerset
Mollie Leadbeater, Brompton Regis
Peter Lee, Wellington
Peter B. Linford,
Daphne M. Lock, Ilfracombe
Mr and Mrs Martyn Lock, Hawkridge
A. Longstaff, Hitchin
John Lowe, Timberscombe
Kevin P. Lynch, Barnstaple
Graham D. Mark, Wiveliscombe
Dr J. E. and Mrs C. A. Marshall, West Down
Mrs E. C. McLaren Throckmorton,
Margaret Melville, Littleham
Creenagh A. Mitchell, Withypool
Mr and Mrs A. G. Mogford, Alston, Cumbria
Bill and Margaret Mogford, Wootton Courtenay,
    Somerset
Wenda Moon, Milverton
Stuart and Linda Morgan, Portsmouth
P. H. Mountford, Orwell
C. C. Muggleton, Wellington
Angela Nation, Stoke Pero
Mr F. C. and Mrs S. R. Newbould, Roachill
Sally Anita Nicholas, Three Legged Cross, Dorset
Sandy and Barbara Noble, Minehead
Francis Northam, Sticklepath
Mrs Rosemarie J. Northcott, South Molton
Dorothy H. Northrop, Torrington, Devon
Kathy Nott, Minehead
Roger W. Notton, East Knowstone
Brian, Alison, Nicola and Philip Palfrey, Rifton,
    Stoodleigh, Devon
Lucy Parrott (née Hosegood), Sherborne

Joan Perry, Crowcombe
Sheila Philp, South Molton
Denis Pickard, Barnstaple
Mrs Blanche Pile, Ilkerton, Lynton
John Pollock, Rose Ash, South Molton, Devon
D. R. and O. M. Poole, Hillcommon
Mr Milns M. Priscott,
Edna H. Pritchard, Minehead
John M. Pruden, Evesham
Lt-Cdr J. A. F. Pugsley R.N., Milverton, Somerset
Jacquelyn F. Pullen, West Monkton
Sybil Rich, Brent Knoll
Olive L. Riches, Farnborough
Kevin Robins, Brayford
Michael E. Robinson, Porlock
John S. Rowe, Minehead, Somerset
Mrs R. G. Rowe, Wiveliscombe, Somerset
Pamela Rowland, Minehead, Somerset
Karen J. Saunders, Brighton, East Sussex
Captain T. J. Sax, Tivington
M. R. Scott, Brendon Hill
C. P. Sharp OBE, Maulden, Bedfordshire
M. J. Shepherd, Southampton
Andrew D. Shepherd, Cumbria
Charles and Diana Sillett, Luckwell Bridge
Basil R. Simmonds, Bampton
Andrew and Patricia Simpson, Fife
Sir Andrew and Lady Sloan
Michael B. Smith, Wiveliscombe
Anne and Bob Smith, Pennymoor
Gillian and Henry Smith
Alison J. Smith, Petton Cross
Patricia Smith, Lamberhurst
Christopher J. Spear, Milltown, Barnstaple
Richard D. J. Spicer, Northam Mill, Stogumber
Hubert (Sherbert) Stevens, late of Exmoor
M. Richard C. G. Swann, Bishops Lydeard
Christopher J. Thacker, Exford
Diana R. T. Tiernan, Chesterfield
Mr and Mrs F. Tovey, Wonham Kiln, Bampton
Stephen Townsend, West Quantoxhead

Mr Jamie S. Trawin Bsc,
Diane M. Vallance, Torquay
D. J. and P. J. Vellacott, Dulverton
Peter G. Vickery, Ilfracombe
Mrs Lorna Vigars
Rita J. Walker, Kingford
Audrey Walker, Dulverton
Doris M. Walker, Wootton Courtenay
John F. Walling, Newton Abbot, Devon
Roger and Jean Waters, Porlock
Barry Watkin, Kingswood, Stogumber
Rodger H. Watts, Filleigh
Andrew Welsh, Dunster
Shirley Wheeler, Oxhey Hall
John N. H. Whitaker, Oxford
Mary E. Whitaker, Dulverton, Somerset
Alwyne White, Brixham, Devon
Douglas White, Cotford St Luke
Hubert R. B. Whittern, Langley Marsh
Mr and Mrs C. H. Williams, Wonham, Bampton,
    Devon
Hilary Williams (Orchard family), Exmoor
Elizabeth and Michael Willison, Uplyme, Devon
Gerald Winzer, Exford
Barbara Wolanowska, Stevenstone
Mr and Mrs R. J. Woollacott, Witheridge
Debbie, Daniel and Rebecca Woollacott, Bampton,
    Devon
Barbara, Clifford, Ian and Andrew Woollacott,
    formerly of Twitchen (Exmoor, Devon)
R. W. Wyatt, Fitzhead
R. H. Wyatt, Croford, Wiveliscombe
C. and S. Wynne, Gratton Barton
Mr Ian G. Yates, Dumfries
George and Julie Yeandle, Chapel Cleeve
Colin Youens, Washford
Richard, Jane, Louise and Thomas Youngman, East
    Village, Devon
Mona van Zwanenberg, Timberscombe